谁是谁·启发精选世界名人传记

U0693634

谁是毕加索

Who Was Pablo Picasso?

〔美〕特鲁·凯利 / 著

〔美〕特鲁·凯利 / 绘

李海颖 / 译

北京联合出版公司

Beijing United Publishing Co.,Ltd.

图书在版编目（CIP）数据

谁是毕加索 ：汉英对照 ／（美）特鲁·凯利著绘 ；
李海颖译. -- 北京 ：北京联合出版公司，2016.11
（谁是谁·启发精选世界名人传记）
ISBN 978-7-5502-8264-3

Ⅰ．①谁… Ⅱ．①特… ②李… Ⅲ．①毕加索，
P.R．（1881-1973）－传记－少儿读物－汉、英 Ⅳ．
①K835.515.72-49

中国版本图书馆CIP数据核字(2016)第167850号

北京市版权局著作权合同登记号：图字01-2016-4447号

Who Was Pablo Picasso?

本简体字版 © 2016由台湾麦克股份有限公司授权出版发行

谁是毕加索
（谁是谁·启发精选世界名人传记）

〔美〕特鲁·凯利/著 〔美〕特鲁·凯利/绘
李海颖/译
选题策划：北京启发世纪图书有限责任公司
台湾麦克股份有限公司
责任编辑：李 伟
特约编辑：朱 菲
美术编辑：刘黎炜

北京联合出版公司
（北京市西城区德外大街83号楼9层 100088）
北京盛通印刷股份有限公司印刷 新华书店经销
字数17千字 880×1230毫米 1/32 印张：5.25
2016年11月第1版 2016年11月第1次印刷
ISBN 978-7-5502-8264-3
定价：19.80元

感谢新罕布什尔州

康科德市和沃纳市的公共图书馆。

——特鲁·凯利

目 录

谁是毕加索？...................................... 1

第一章　小神童 6

第二章　年轻的艺术家 16

第三章　巴黎的生活 23

第四章　毕加索的惊世画作 35

第五章　新的尝试 44

第六章　不断坠入情网 51

第七章　战争与和平 72

第八章　坛坛罐罐 82

第九章　忙碌的晚年 91

毕加索年表 102

世界大事年表 103

词汇表 162

Contents

Who Was Pablo Picasso? 107

Chapter 1   The Boy Wonder 110

Chapter 2   The Young Artist 115

Chapter 3   Life in Paris 120

Chapter 4   Pablo's Shocking Paintings 126

Chapter 5   Something New 131

Chapter 6   Falling in Love Again and Again 135

Chapter 7   War and Peace 144

Chapter 8   Pots and Pans 150

Chapter 9   Busy to the End 153

Timeline of Pablo Picasso's Life 158

Timeline of the World 159

Bibliography 160

Vocabulary 162

谁是毕加索？

想到现代艺术时，第一个闪现在你脑海中的名字或许就是毕加索。如果没有他，当今的艺术将是另一种面貌！

巴勃罗·毕加索的一生漫长而有趣。他经历了两次世界大战，目睹了电力、电话、收音机、电视机、电影、汽车和飞机的问世。当世界发展变化时，他也总能随之改变自己。

　　毕加索创作过各种类型的艺术作品，数量也很庞大。他每天勤奋工作，持续了八十多年。有人说他创作的艺术品有五万件之多！他一定拥有超级充沛的精力。

　　他创作的作品有油画、海报、石质和金属的雕

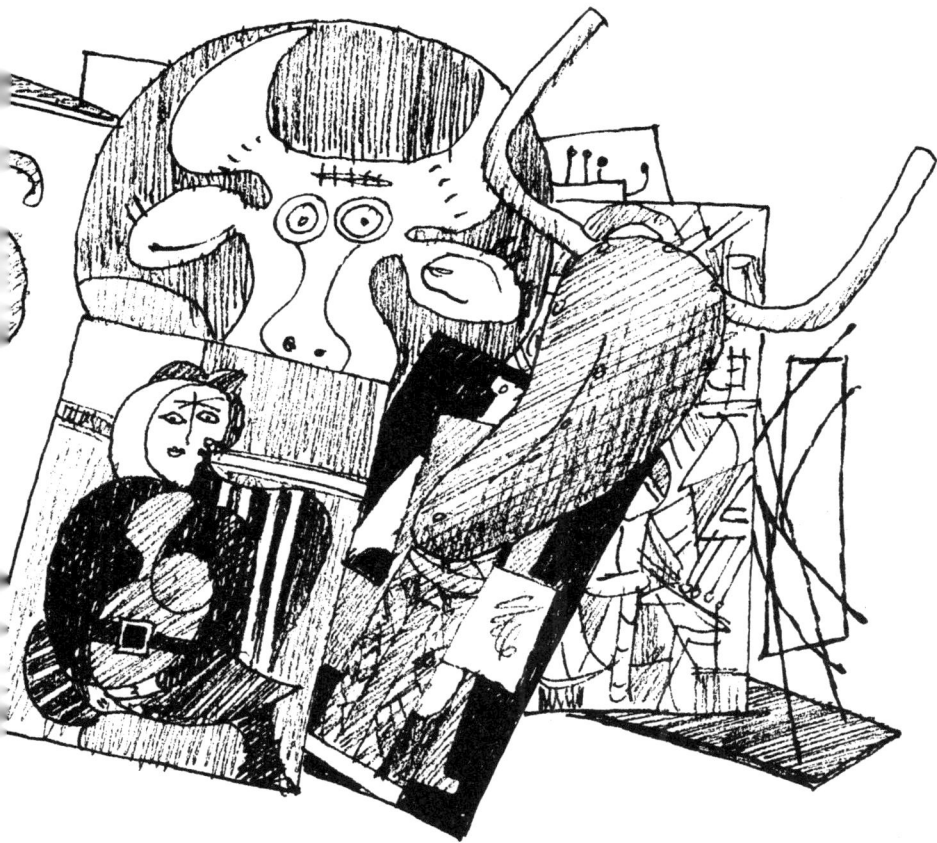

塑、陶器、素描、拼贴画、版画、诗歌、舞台布景
和舞台服装等等。毕加索总能不断想出新点子。他
喜欢创新又技艺娴熟，一旦掌握了一种风格，就会
去尝试另一种。因此，他的画风比其他任何一位大
艺术家都富于变化。

与许多艺术家不同的是，毕加索很成功，而且他成名得很快。他总是知道如何引起人们的关注。在九岁那年，毕加索就开始出售自己的画了。当他九十一岁去世时，他已是历史上最富有的艺术家。

毕加索通过自己的艺术作品，传达了有关政治、社会、和平和爱情的强烈讯息。因为毕加索的缘故，鸽子被人们视为和平的象征。他的名画《格尔尼卡》表现了战争的恐怖和残暴。

毕加索的艺术作品时而严肃，时而幽默；时而天真，时而现实；时而鲜艳，时而灰暗；时而简单，时而复杂。他还是个孩子时，就能像才华横溢的成年人一样画画了。不过，年纪越大，他反而越想像小孩子一样进行艺术创作。

1939年创作的《逮住小鸟的猫》

第一章　小神童

1881 年 10 月 25 日，在西班牙南部城市马拉加，一位美术教师和妻子生下了一个男孩。夫妻俩用了很多圣徒和家族成员的名字来给儿子取名，他的全名叫：巴勃罗·迭戈·何塞·弗朗西斯科·德保拉·胡安·内波穆塞诺·玛丽亚·德洛斯雷梅迪奥斯·西普里亚诺·德

毕加索的母亲

毕加索的父亲

拉桑蒂西玛·特立尼达·鲁伊斯－毕加索。许多年以后，这个孩子成了一位众人皆知的大艺术家，他就是巴勃罗·毕加索。他怎样才能在画作上签下自己的全名呢？那根本做不到！所以，他只写"毕加索"。

还不会说话的时候，毕加索就会画画了。他的母亲说，他讲的第一句话是"Piz! Piz!"这是西班牙语单词"lapiz"的儿语，意思是"铅笔"。在他很小很小的时候，他喜欢画螺旋的形状。有时，他会在沙地上画画。

　　如果要画一匹马，他可以从任意一点开始，无论是马尾还是马腿，然后一笔画出一幅非常棒的图画。即使是用剪刀和纸，他也能做到同样的事。你们尝试过吗？这可不容易呢！

毕加索的父母希望他成为一名艺术家。还是个小男孩的时候，他经常跟着父亲去看斗牛表演。毕加索第一幅出名的画作描绘的就是一场斗牛。他画那幅画时，大概还只有八岁。每个人都认为毕加索是个艺术天才——他们没有看错。

四岁的毕加索

毕加索有两个妹妹，洛拉和孔奇塔。遗憾的是，在他年纪还小的时候，七岁的孔奇塔就因为得了白喉病夭折了。全家人都受到了沉重的打击。从那以后，毕加索便对死亡心存恐惧。

孔奇塔

洛拉

十三岁那年，毕加索举办了第一场个人艺术展。这时，毕加索的父亲发现儿子比自己画得更好。于是，他的父亲把自己所有的画笔和颜料都给了儿子，从此再没有画过画。

毕加索和家人搬到了巴塞罗那，这是一个艺术家云集、令人心潮澎湃的城市。毕加索被当地一所艺术学校录取了，他的父亲就在这所学校教绘画。

十五岁的毕加索

虽然当时只有十四岁，毕加索却跳过了基础课程而直接学起高级课程。他的才华让老师们大为惊讶！

　　十六岁那年，毕加索的艺术生涯才真正开始。他创作了一幅名为《科学与仁慈》的油画，他的父亲和妹妹是模特儿。在这幅画上，妹妹洛拉被画成卧床的病患，父亲被画成医生坐在床边。这幅油画有着强烈的现实主义风格。它在马德里的一场展览上获奖。毕加索超越了不少西班牙最优秀的画家！

1897 年创作的《科学与仁慈》

毕加索的家人认为他会成为一位了不起的艺术家。他们把他送到马德里，在圣费尔南多皇家学院学习艺术。这是一所公认的好学校，但毕加索却经常逃课。他的老师要求他临摹其他绘画和雕塑，但他认为这种教学方法毫无用处并且已经过时了。结果，大把的时间都被他用来泡咖啡馆了。他

还非常爱去著名的普拉多艺术博物馆，在那里他看到了西班牙大师埃尔·格列柯和弗朗西斯科·戈雅的作品。

毕加索在西班牙的生活

毕加索和他的家人从西班牙南部的马拉加——毕加索的出生地——搬到了西班牙北部的拉科鲁尼亚，然后又搬去了巴塞罗那。在那之后，毕加索前往马德里学习艺术。他生病以后，去了一个名叫奥尔塔·德圣胡安的小村庄。然后，他又回到巴塞罗那，但却抵抗不了巴黎对他的诱惑。

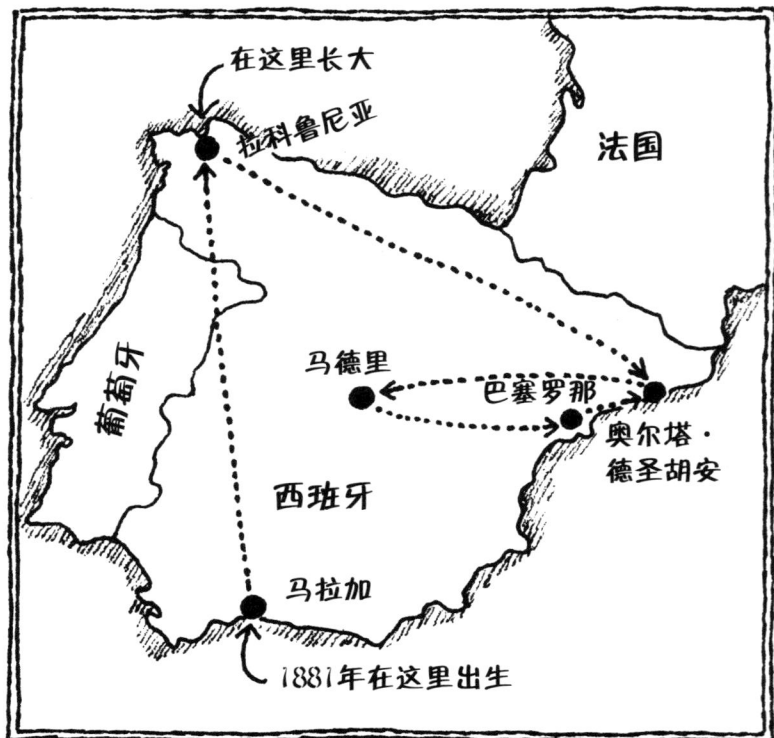

在这里长大

拉科鲁尼亚

法国

马德里

巴塞罗那

奥尔塔·德圣胡安

葡萄牙

西班牙

马拉加

1881年在这里出生

到了冬天，毕加索因为猩红热而病倒了。他离开学校去了一个小村庄，在那里一直住到身体好转。关于自己的未来，他思考了很久。毕加索决定不回学校了，他还决定要用自己的方式来作画。他的家人不会赞成他的想法，但跃跃欲试的毕加索已经准备好要走自己的路。

第二章　年轻的艺术家

十八岁
的毕加索

　　毕加索回到巴塞罗那，在那里经常和一帮艺术家、诗人、作家光顾一家名叫"四只猫"的咖啡馆。他们称自己为"现代派艺术家"。1900年，毕加索在这家咖啡馆举办了他的第一场个人画展。他展出了五十多幅为友人及家人画的肖像画，还有将近六十幅素描和油画。有一幅画的是一位牧师，他站在一个垂死女人的床边。这幅画获邀在巴黎举行的世界博览会上展出。毕加索正需要这样一个去巴黎的理由。与他一起去的还有一位在美术学校结识的老朋友——卡莱斯·卡萨吉马斯。

毕加索和卡莱斯没有钱。他们住的公寓没有家具，于是毕加索在墙上画了家具和书架，这样房间才不显得那么空荡荡。他甚至在墙上画了一个保险柜，好像他们真有什么贵重东西能放进去似的。

不过，房子并不重要，他们已经在巴黎了！这里可是艺术界和时尚界的中心。巴黎活力四射，而毕加索精力充沛！他在这里看到了莫奈、德加、塞尚、梵高、高更、图卢兹－劳特累克的艺术作品。五彩缤纷的巴黎很快让毕加索的绘画也变得色彩斑斓。他花了两个月来画巴黎的风景，还卖出了三幅描绘斗牛的蜡笔画，这是令人振奋的成绩。

毕加索很喜欢巴黎，但可怜的卡莱斯这时却伤心欲绝，他的女朋友离他而去了。所以，卡莱斯和毕加索又回到了毕加索在西班牙的故乡。当毕加索走进家门时，他的家人可不喜欢他的模样！瞧他的穿着打扮！还有那长长的头发！家人们断定毕加索是在虚掷光阴。

于是，毕加索去了马德里。他帮别人办了一份美术杂志，还为杂志创作反映穷人悲惨状况的政治漫画。他将朋友卡莱斯留在了家乡，这时卡莱斯依然极度消沉而且很难相处。不久后，卡莱斯回到了

卡莱斯·卡萨吉马斯

巴黎。他此时已经一筹莫展、不知所措了。他先是试图向前女友开枪，之后开枪打死了自己。

毕加索震惊不已。他可能也为自己抛下痛苦不堪的朋友而感到内疚。卡莱斯的死影响了毕加索的绘画，他画了两幅色彩灰暗的葬礼画和两幅卡莱斯

的死者肖像画。然后，他开始用蓝色来作画。

毕加索说："对卡莱斯的怀念让我开始用蓝色来画画。"1901年，他完成了一幅自画像，整幅画基本上都是蓝色的。画上的他看起来很忧郁。后来，这个时期被称为毕加索的"蓝色时期"。

1901年创作的《穿斗篷的自画像》

从 1901 年至 1904 年，毕加索辗转往返于巴塞罗那和巴黎之间。他住在廉价的旅馆和破败的公寓里。毕加索与诗人马克斯·雅各布合租一间公寓。他们只买得起一张床，于是毕加索白天在床上睡觉，马克斯晚上在床上睡觉。毕加索在夜里工作，他的余生也一直保留着这个习惯。

因为经常没钱买画布和颜料，毕加索画了许多素描。乞丐、盲人、孤独的人和犯人都是他的绘画题材。毕加索很关心这些人。为了寻找模特儿，他去过巴黎的一所女子监狱。终其一生，毕加索都热衷于画女子。

时间到了 1903 年。仅用了一年多一点儿的时间，毕加索就完成了五十幅用蓝、绿色调创作的油画。可是没人愿意买它们，人们不想把这么压抑的画挂在自家墙上。毕加索的父亲和许多朋友都认定，毕加索画这些奇怪的蓝色画是误入歧途。

可是毕加索会听他们的劝告吗？不，他只做自己想做的事！

1903年创作的《弹吉他的老人》（蓝色调）

第三章 巴黎的生活

毕加索，
1904年

　　是什么让毕加索走出了他的"蓝色时期"？回到巴黎（这次是长期的回归）是原因之一。生机勃勃的巴黎在毕加索身上施展了魔法，他变得快乐多了。他开始以流动马戏团的杂耍演员和杂技演员为主角，创作色彩缤纷的油画。他们都是社会边缘人，就像毕加索在"蓝色时期"画过的那些人一样。

《杂技演员一家》

　　毕加索在创作油画《杂技演员一家》时下了一番苦功。他以费尔南德和一位朋友为模特儿来画马戏团一家人。人们用 X 射线研究这幅画，发现毕加索至少完整地画了四次，才画成他满意的样子。

让毕加索的"蓝色时期"结束的另一个原因，是他交了一个新女朋友。她是位美丽的艺术家，名叫费尔南德·奥利维尔。毕加索的画作展现了

毕加索、费尔南德和他们的宠物狗，1906年

他的幸福，这个时期有时被称为毕加索的"玫瑰时期"。不过，他的绘画里有许多种颜色，不仅仅是粉红色。

毕加索的宠物

毕加索一生养过许多宠物，有一只温顺的小白鼠、一只乌龟、一只山羊和一只猴子。毕加索非常喜欢狗，当他还是一个穷困潦倒的艺术家时，就养了一条又大又可爱的老狗，狗的名字叫弗里卡。有一次，毕加索没有食物了，弗里卡竟拖着一串香肠跑进家门！毕加索平生最喜欢的宠物可能是一条名叫兰普的腊肠犬。在德语里，"兰普"是"淘气鬼"的意思。在戏仿名画《宫娥》时，毕加索把兰普画了上去，取代了原作中委拉斯开兹画的那条样貌高贵的猎犬。

埃斯梅拉达

扬

加特

卡斯贝克

兰普

　　毕加索和费尔南德住在一幢庞大而破旧的公
寓楼里，这里住的都是艺术家和诗人。他俩的房间
很潮湿，又脏又乱，到处堆着毕加索还未完成的作
品。毕加索不愿丢弃任何东西。他说："为什么要我
扔掉那些从天而降、落到我手心里的好东西呢？"

他们有一条名叫弗里卡的大黄狗，还在梳妆台的抽屉里养了一只宠物小白鼠。毕加索喜欢夜里在油灯下工作。他经常工作到清晨五六点钟。冬天的时候，屋里有时特别冷，连没喝完的茶水都会冻住。

就在这个时期，毕加索在巴黎遇到了许多有趣的人物。在他们眼中，毕加索也是一个有趣的人。他很热情，也很深奥。他魅力非凡，而且他的好奇心、活力、才智和创造力也很引人关注。尽管个子

毕加索和朋友们在咖啡馆里

矮小，身高只有一米六，但他拥有一双目光锐利的黑眼睛，毕加索看上去还是非常俊朗的。

他遇到了一个名叫格特鲁德·斯泰因的富裕的美国女人和她的哥哥利奥。格特鲁德是一位诗人，

利奥·斯泰因

格特鲁德·斯泰因

"玫瑰就是玫瑰就是玫瑰就是玫瑰"是她笔下的名句。她是最早赏识毕加索绘画的人之一，曾经买过毕加索的一些画。

周六晚上，诗人和艺术家们在斯泰因位于巴黎的寓所聚会。毕加索在这里遇到了画家亨利·马蒂斯。毕加索认为马蒂斯是当时最伟大的画家，他曾说过："总而言之，我只在乎马蒂斯。"虽然是竞争对手，但他们却成了一生的朋友。

马蒂斯、格特鲁德·斯泰因和毕加索在巴黎

格特鲁德·斯泰因的肖像画

1906 年，毕加索为格特鲁德画了一幅肖像画。这次创作让毕加索倍受煎熬，因为他总是画不好她的脸。为了这幅肖像画，格特鲁德前前后后坐下来八十次当模特儿！对她来说，这或许也是一种折磨！夏天的时候，毕加索弃笔不画了；到了秋天，他又凭着自己的记忆来画她的脸。他画的脸看起来就像一个原始人的面具。毕加索曾经在一家博物馆见过非洲艺术和原始艺术，所以他才会这样画。他从不畏惧借用其他的概念。

一个木制的
非洲人面具

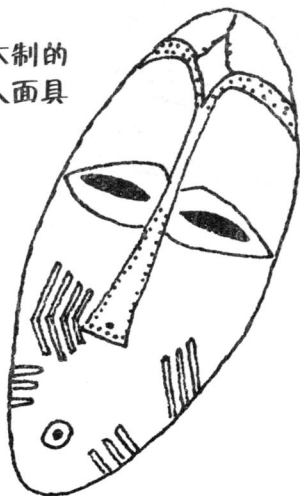

一个原始时期的
伊比利亚雕塑

人们认为这幅画画得一点儿都不像格特鲁德，但她本人却很喜欢。她说："在我看来，这就是我。"

完成了格特鲁德·斯泰因的肖像画以后，毕加索意识到他不必一五一十地描绘自己所见的事物，他可以根据自己的想象来作画。这是毕加索创作道路上的一个转折点，也是现代艺术史上的一个转折点！

第四章 毕加索的惊世画作

　　1907 年，毕加索完成了他到那时为止画过的最大的油画：约两米四高、两米四宽。这幅画上有五个女人，其中一个女人的头好像旋转了一百八十度。这幅画叫作《亚维农的少女》。

《亚维农的少女》

按当时的标准来看，这幅画实在太狂野了。画上的五个女人看起来棱角突出，非常扭曲。她们真难看！她们的形体好像支离破碎了。

　　人们认为这幅画应该画得更写实一点儿。它太令人不安、太吓人了！从来没人画过这样的画。创作这幅画改变了毕加索对绘画的理解。毕加索用了数个月的时间来完成这幅画。为了画它，毕加索画了许多许多草图（总共有八百零九张！）。他知道自己违反了所有的绘画规则，但他想要同时从多个角度来描绘女性，就像观众同时从不同方向打量她们一样。

非洲部落的面具

毕加索画的女性

人人都讨厌这幅画！有一位评论家称它为"疯子的作品"。毕加索把这幅画收起来，有九年时间没有让它露面。虽然博得公众关注是好事，但他的感情还是受到了伤害。

如今，这幅画被称为 20 世纪的第一幅现代画。毕加索找到了一种新的观察方法。

有一个人真心喜欢毕加索的创新风格。他是位画廊老板，名叫 D. H. 坎魏勒。他成为了毕加索的艺术经纪人和密友。

D.H.坎魏勒

毕加索的另一位密友是艺术家乔治·布拉克。毕加索和布拉克发现，他们俩的想法非常相似。

乔治·布拉克

他们都深受保罗·塞尚的绘画作品的影响。

保罗·塞尚的《埃斯塔克之海》

有五年的时间，毕加索和布拉克天天见面。他们甚至一起去度假。他们一起创作，关系如此紧密，以至于毕加索说，有时连他们自己都分不清哪幅画是谁画的。他们会看彼此的作品，共同决定一幅画是否画好了。布拉克说，他和毕加索就像绑在同一根绳上的两个登山者。后来，毕加索再也没有与别的艺术家这么紧密地合作过。

布拉克和毕加索创作静物画、风景画和肖像画。他们使用的颜色都很少，并把画中的对象分解成立方体和几何图形。他们试图在同一时间、全方位地描绘出他们的对象。毕加索说："我是依我所想来画对象，而不是依我所见来画。"他们共同开创了一种新的绘画风格——立体主义！

1910年创作的《安布鲁瓦兹·沃拉尔的肖像画》

　　在毕加索一生创作的所有重要艺术作品中，让他声名鹊起的是立体主义作品。一开始，立体主义让人们感到震惊，因为他们从没见过这样的作品。

但是不久后，人们发现其实他们喜欢这样的风格！

毕加索说："我知道我们画的东西很奇怪，但在我们看来，这个世界就是这样一个奇怪的地方。"

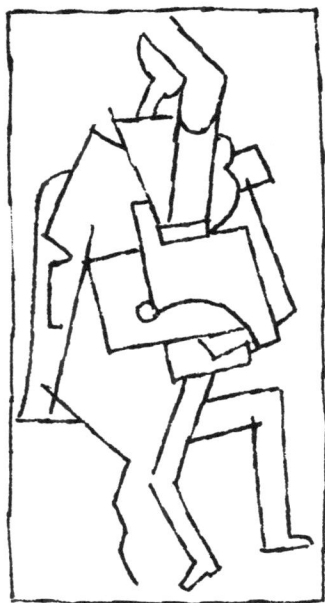

普通的素描　　　　　　　立体主义素描

第五章　新的尝试

二十六岁的毕加索，1907年

　　到 1909 年，毕加索已经远近闻名了。他的绘画与众不同，但人们还是不断买他的画。他和费尔南德搬进了一所更漂亮的房子，他们还雇了一个女仆。夏天，他们和布拉克一起住在山间一幢旧别墅

费尔南德·奥利维尔

里消夏。之后，毕加索和费尔南德的关系破裂了。毕加索说："她的美貌让我倾心，但我不能忍受她的那些小毛病。"很快，毕加索有了一位新女友，她叫埃娃·古埃尔。毕加索

埃娃·古埃尔

为埃娃画了一幅画，题为《我的美人》。毕加索又恋爱了。在他漫长的一生中，毕加索多次坠入情网。

1912年创作的《我的美人》

毕加索和布拉克再次开始新尝试。他们将镂花模板和印刷文字应用到画作中。他们还开始往自己的画里粘贴其他物件。如果想表现一张报纸，他们不会画出这张报纸，而是直接贴上一张真的报纸。这就是拼贴画的起源，拼贴的意思就是"粘贴"。《有藤椅的静物》是毕加索最早的拼贴画之一。

毕加索的拼贴画中使用的材料

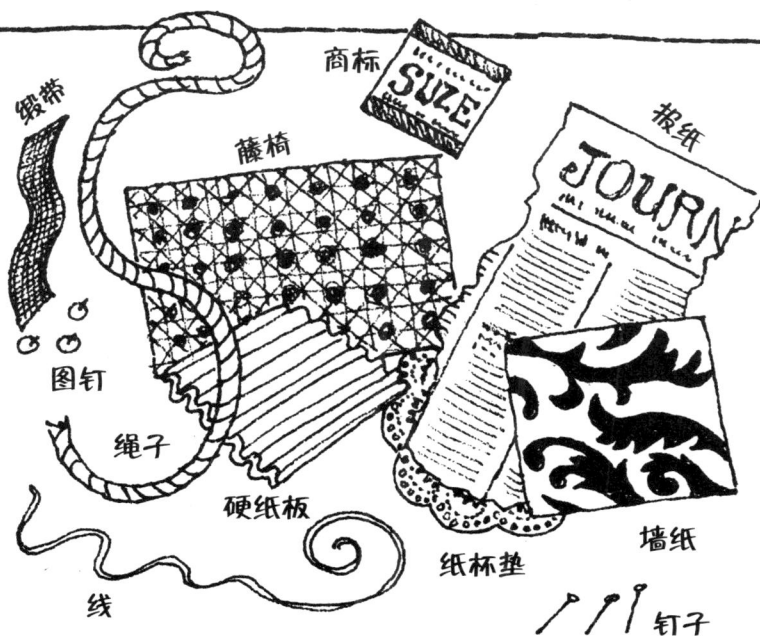

缎带
商标
SIZE
藤椅
报纸
JOURN
图钉
绳子
硬纸板
纸杯垫
墙纸
线
钉子

布拉克和毕加索继续以他们游戏的方式往画作上贴东西：布片、砂纸、墙纸，甚至还有垃圾！

可是，他们的艺术实验却被世界大事打断了。1914 年，奥匈帝国和塞尔维亚之间的局部战争升级演变成了大战——第一次世界大战。一个塞尔维亚人刺杀了奥地利大公，德国支持奥匈帝国，俄国支持塞尔维亚。德国向俄国宣战，然后又向法国宣战。很快，世界各国都卷入到战争之中，美国也未能置身事外。

1914 年，布拉克被征募进入法国军队。毕加索不是法国公民，所以他不必参军。他的许多朋友奔赴前线去打仗了，而他留在了巴黎。毕加索很想念他们。

法国当时正与德国交战。毕加索的朋友、画廊主人坎魏勒因为是德国人，所以被迫离开法国。（法国人认为所有德国人都是敌人。）坎魏勒的画廊被法国当局关闭了，毕加索放在那里的所有作品都被没收了。

1915 年，毕加索挚爱的埃娃因为肺结核去世了。毕加索伤心欲绝。他的画作再一次表现了他内心的悲伤。埃娃生病的时候，他一直在画《小丑》，这幅画直到埃娃死后才完成。这幅画画的是一个小丑模样的艺术家，他站在画架前，手里拿着一幅尚未完成的画作。《小丑》这幅画的背景是黑色的。这段岁月是欧洲历史上也是毕加索人生中一段灰暗的时光。

第六章　不断坠入情网

三十六岁的
毕加索，
1917年

　　一战期间，毕加索在巴黎认识了一些新朋友。其中一位是诗人、剧作家让·科克托。他将毕加索介绍给一位作曲家认识。他们俩说服毕加索为一部在罗马上演的芭蕾舞剧设计舞台布景和演出服装。这部剧讲的是一个马戏团的故事，剧名叫《巡游》。毕加索以前还从没看过芭蕾舞剧呢！为了这个工

作，他去了罗马。等到最终上演时，《巡游》引发
了轩然大波。对大多数人来说，这部剧太与众不同
了，演出服装也太狂野了。

芭蕾舞演员！

法国经理的戏服　　　　美国经理的戏服

还有那些舞台布景……音乐……和舞蹈，也都
同样狂野。

Programme des Ballets Russes

芭蕾舞剧
的节目单

马的戏服

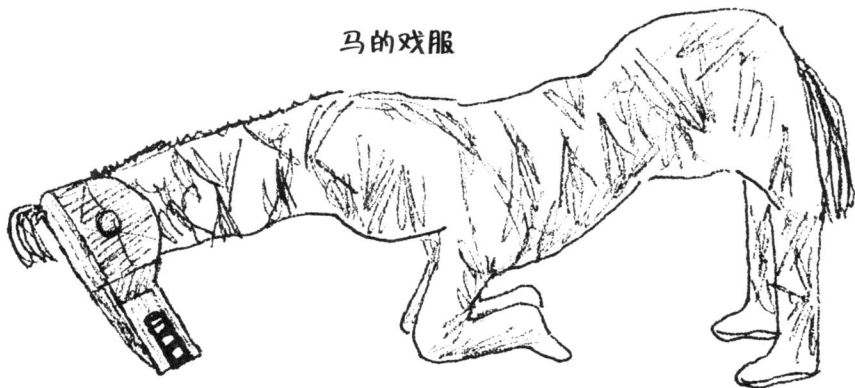

1917年创作的《奥尔加》

在罗马的时候，毕加索迷上了古希腊和古罗马艺术。他也迷上了美丽的奥尔加·霍赫洛娃，她是《巡游》里的一位芭蕾舞演员。一年以后，他和她结婚了。

回到巴黎后，奥尔加将毕加索引荐进入了上流社会。他们出席正式的舞会，去时髦的度假胜地。对于像毕加索这样一向非常关心穷人的人，这是一个很大的转变。奥尔加是个势利的人，她让毕加索远离往日的老朋友，毕加索听从了。他不再需要工作，因为他已经变得富有。不过，这并不意味着他停止了工作。他只是再一次转变了方向。

20世纪20年代，毕加索和奥尔加在一场化装舞会上

战争结束后，毕加索创作的立体主义作品和拼贴画大幅减少。他重新开始用比较传统的方式来作画。经过一系列的艺术实验，毕加索找到了另一种让世人惊讶的方式——不做人们所期待的毕加索！

1921 年，毕加索和奥尔加有了一个儿子，名叫保罗。毕加索很宠爱他的小宝宝。他喜欢做父亲的感觉，但这对他来说是一个很大的变化。

两岁的保罗

他一次次地用新的风格来描绘母亲和儿子。这些画里的形状很稳固，不像在他的立体主义作品中那样参差不齐、支离破碎。

他的画作《春天里的三个女人》描绘了三个穿着希腊古典服饰的人物。她们的身体线条很圆润，腿很粗。毕加索说，画她们的腿让他想起年幼时在餐桌下爬来爬去，看到姨妈们脚踝的童年记忆。

在同一时期，他还用非常简化的立体主义风格
画了《三个音乐家》。不过，这时画里的形状和颜色
都变得明亮多了。画上的人物看起来就像拼图玩具里
的拼板。为什么毕加索会突然从一种风格换成另一
种呢？他说自己只是想采用最适合主题的风格而已。

1919年，毕加索
在画室里

之后，毕加索开始画半人半马和半人半羊之类的形象。在意大利时，他在古代雕塑和绘画上看到过它们，非常喜欢。

半人半马

半人半羊

立体主义艺术家认为毕加索背离了立体主义。但毕加索不在乎其他艺术家的看法。他不想自己被别人贴上标签。他可是毕加索！

到了 1925 年，毕加索对艺术和文学领域的超现实主义运动产生了兴趣。超现实主义绘画是一种

1932年创作的《红色扶手椅中的女人》

表现人的潜意识的画法。

毕加索画出了一个充满幻梦和噩梦的世界。他参加了一场超现实主义艺术展。此外，毕加索写诗、为图书绘制插图，还制作蚀刻版画。他一个人的精力可以抵十个人！

毕加索很多超现实主义画作和蚀刻版画都是以斗牛为主题的。他还创作了许多米诺陶的形象，米诺陶是人们想象中的一种半人半牛的生物。有些艺术评论家认为，毕加索喜欢把自己想象成一只米诺陶！

米诺陶

制作蚀刻版画

蚀刻版画是用锋利的工具在金属板上雕刻出来的画，然后用这块金属板来印制图像。

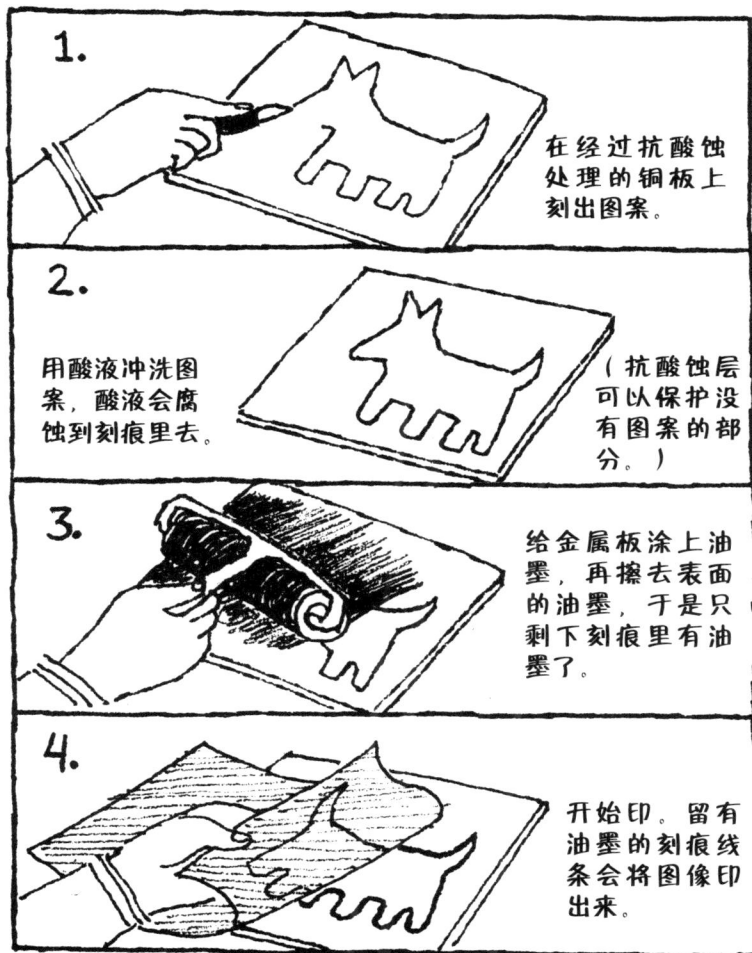

1. 在经过抗酸蚀处理的铜板上刻出图案。

2. 用酸液冲洗图案，酸液会腐蚀到刻痕里去。

（抗酸蚀层可以保护没有图案的部分。）

3. 给金属板涂上油墨，再擦去表面的油墨，于是只剩下刻痕里有油墨了。

4. 开始印。留有油墨的刻痕线条会将图像印出来。

毕加索也对制作雕塑产生了兴趣。他完成了一些以吉他为主题的拼贴画，使用了许多立体的物品，如钉子、线和布片等。这样的拼贴画就像变成了雕塑一样。

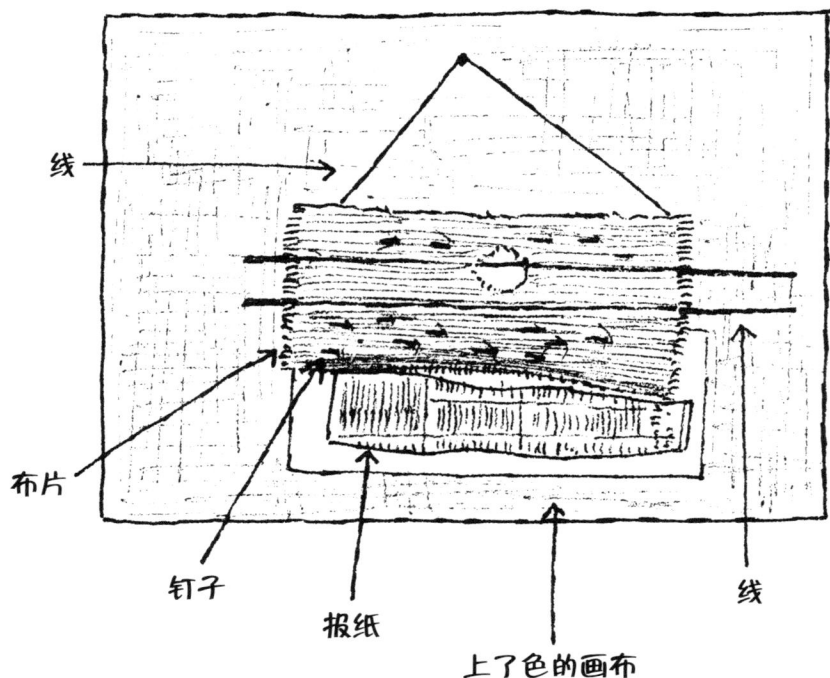

1926年创作的《吉他》

线

布片

钉子

报纸

上了色的画布

线

有一天，毕加索在巴黎遇到一位金属工匠，他同时也是位雕刻家。他叫胡利奥·冈萨雷斯，也是西班牙人。胡利奥和毕加索成为了朋友。他们一起用焊接的铁棒和铁丝来创作抽象雕塑，这是一种全新的尝试。

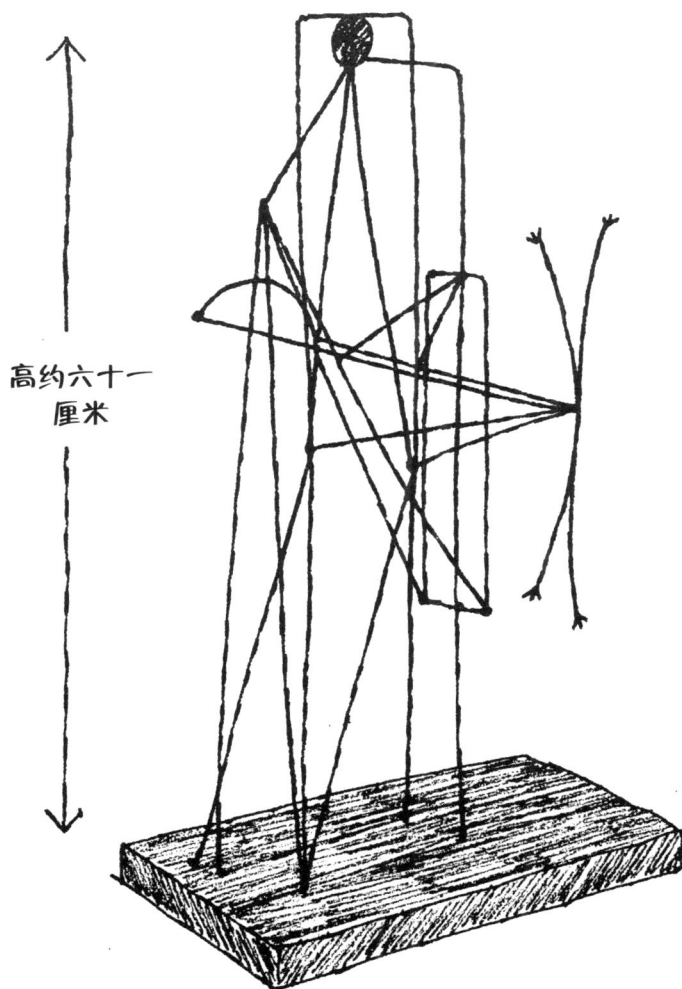

高约六十一
厘米

1920年，毕加索乱糟糟的画室

令人遗憾的是，毕加索与奥尔加的婚姻破裂了。在家里，他们各自住在不同的楼层。奥尔加很讨厌毕加索那个乱糟糟的画室（它又脏又乱！），但毕加索却说混乱能够激发他的灵感。现在，奥尔加成了一个麻烦。毕加索说："她对我的要求太多了。"于是，他在巴黎北部买了一所大房子来躲避她。毕加索说，他与奥尔加共同生活的最后几个月就像一场噩梦。

毕加索在新住所的马厩里建起了一个雕塑工作室。他制作了大型的石膏头像，并开始用奇怪的材料来做雕塑。在创作雕塑《一个女子的头部》时甚至使用了滤锅。

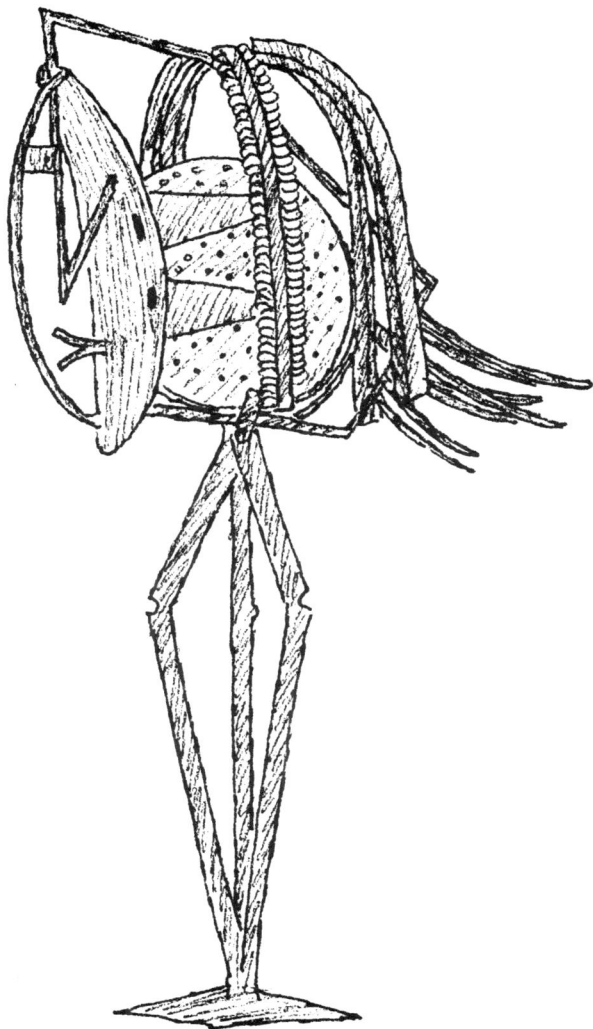

毕加索遇到了一个年轻姑娘，当时她正从巴黎地铁的出口往外走。她叫玛丽-泰蕾兹·瓦尔特。他们俩一见钟情。毕加索马上开始为她作画。几年后，毕加索和玛丽-泰蕾兹生了一个女儿，取名为玛雅。他们此后一直幸福地生活在一起了吗？没有！

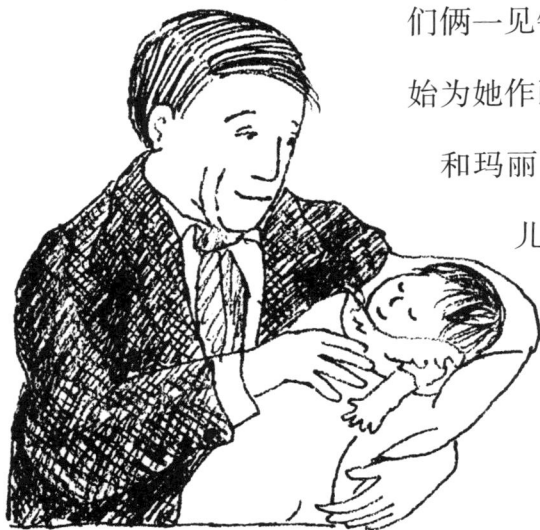

1936年的多
拉·马尔

毕加索后来遇见了一位名叫多拉·马尔的摄影师。他的女儿出生才一年，他就爱上了多拉。毕加索好像很享受错综复杂的爱情生活。他一边仍在和玛丽-泰蕾兹约会，一边与奥尔加周旋，现在又出现了多拉。

毕加索的灵感女神——他生命中的女人们

毕加索对女性来说很有吸引力，但和他生活在一起肯定不容易！他的脾气不好，在创作不顺的时候会很暴躁。当然，在其他时候，他是非常有魅力的。他爱女人，但他非常以自我为中心，而且十分

1904年遇见
费尔南德

1911年遇见
埃娃

1917年遇
见奥尔加

1927年遇见
玛丽-泰蕾兹

Ma
Jolie

1921年儿子
保罗出生

1935年女儿
玛雅出生

专注于自己的艺术。在他的人生中，他有过很多女朋友和妻子，还生了四个孩子。她们既是他的模特儿，也是他最主要的灵感来源，对他具有重要的意义。我们知道这些女子的模样，因为他把她们都画进了画里。她们都很美丽。

1936年遇见多拉

1944年遇见弗朗索瓦丝

1953年遇见杰奎琳

1947年儿子克劳德出生

1949年女儿帕洛玛出生

第七章 战争与和平

　　有些艺术家只用一种风格画一种题材的画。可是，毕加索却一直在改变。毕加索的绘画既反映了他个人生活中发生的事，也反映了外部世界的发展变化。

1936 年，西班牙内战爆发。毕加索当时住在巴黎，但他还是深受西班牙战争的影响。毕竟，他是西班牙人。

在西班牙，人民选举产生了一个共和政府。但是，这个政府被弗朗西斯科·佛朗哥将军和他的军

佛朗哥将军

队推翻了。佛朗哥是个独裁者，他一直统治着西班牙，直到他 1975 年去世。因为佛朗哥，毕加索再也没有回到自己的祖国。

1937 年 4 月，西班牙东北部的小城格尔尼卡遭到了德军的轰炸，德军支持的是佛朗哥及其党羽。格尔尼卡距毕加索的家乡不远。轰炸发生在赶集的日子，一千六百多人——其中有男有女，还有儿童——因此丧命，还有近九百人受伤。这场袭击没有任何军事原因。

毕加索对这起屠杀广大无辜平民的事件感到非常愤慨。怀着满腔义愤，他画了一幅高三米七长七米九的油画，题为《格尔尼卡》。这幅画是毕加索最著名的画作。他仅用三周时间就完成了。他的新女友多拉拍摄了许多他创作这幅油画时的照片。

这幅画以灰暗的色调刻画了嘶叫的马匹、倒地的士兵、从着火的房子上尖叫着跌落下来的妇女，还有一位怀抱死婴的母亲。画上有一条握剑的断臂和一个被砍下的头颅。在这片混乱之中，还站着一头牛，也许它象征的是战胜佛朗哥的希望。《格尔尼卡》强有力地描绘了战争的恐怖，这种描绘也非常令人不安。

　　当别人请他解释这幅画的含义时，毕加索说："不应该由画家来定义这些符号的寓意。否则，还不如让画家用一大堆文字把寓意写出来算了！"

　　然后到了 1939 年，德国军队入侵波兰，第二次世界大战爆发了。因为害怕轰炸，巴黎的博物馆纷纷关闭了。许多艺术品被转移到乡村藏匿起来。许多艺术家逃离了这座城市。毕加索和他的家人也离开了巴黎。他们搬到了鲁瓦扬，那是一个濒临大西洋的法国小城。

1940 年，德军占领了巴黎。毕加索决定回到他在巴黎的画室。他为什么要这么做？

或许毕加索希望，在法国人民心中，他的坚守能成为一个骄傲的、代表抗争与自由的象征。

巴黎的食物供应越来越紧张，所以有时毕加索会画一些香肠和韭菜的画。尽管美术用品的供应也很匮乏，但毕加索还是设法每天画画。他还写了一个剧本。纳粹分子不赞同他的任何作品。不过，这并不能阻止毕加索！

毕加索对多拉的爱消退了，他遇到了一位名叫弗朗索瓦丝·吉洛的年轻艺术家，从此开始了一段长达十年的感情生活。

1944 年，纳粹终于被赶出巴黎。毕加索继续作画，他一边画画一边大声唱歌，用歌声来掩盖外面的枪炮声。德国军队刚刚离开，巴黎就举行了一场庆祝会。巴黎重获自由，战争就要结束了。

1943年的弗朗索瓦丝·吉洛

　　美国士兵蜂拥进入巴黎。据说，他们最想做的两件事就是参观埃菲尔铁塔和去见毕加索！毕加索乐意让人们参观自己的画室，这里欢迎所有人。有些士兵到来时已经很疲惫，他们甚至在那儿睡着了。有一次，有人数出来有二十名士兵在毕加索的画室里睡觉！

美国军队进入解放后的巴黎

第二次世界大战持续了六年。到这时，毕加索已经经历了三场战争。他深知为和平而努力是多么重要。1948年，他出席了在波兰举行的和平大会。第二年，他为和平大会制作了一张画有鸽子的海报。因为毕加索的缘故，如今鸽子在世界各地都已成为和平的象征。

世界保卫
和平大会

普莱耶尔音乐厅
1949年4月20、21、22、23日
巴黎

第八章　坛坛罐罐

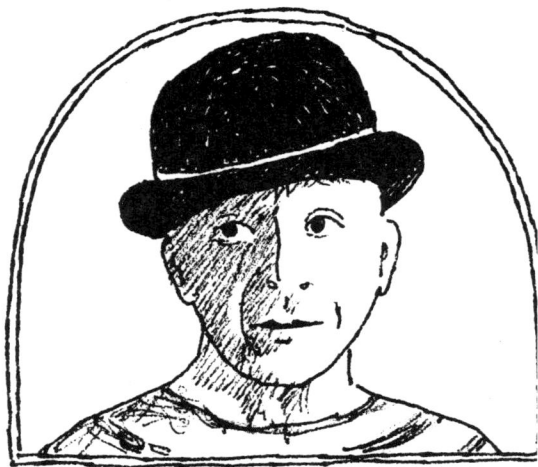

1955年的毕加索

　　战争结束后，毕加索和弗朗索瓦丝搬到了法国南部的小城瓦洛里。他们住在一个老香水工厂里，有一个房间用作雕塑工作室。他们的两个孩子都出生在瓦洛里——儿子克劳德生于 1947 年，女儿帕

1952年，毕加索、弗朗索瓦丝以及他们
的孩子克劳德和帕洛玛

洛玛（意思是"鸽子"）生于 1949 年。

这座小城还有一间陶艺厂。毕加索开始和陶艺

工人一起工作，烧制陶器、盘子和花瓶，并给它们

绘上图案和颜色。

起初，他只是在陶艺工人做好的陶器上绘图。但很快他就自己制作陶器了。他的设计既欢乐又有趣。

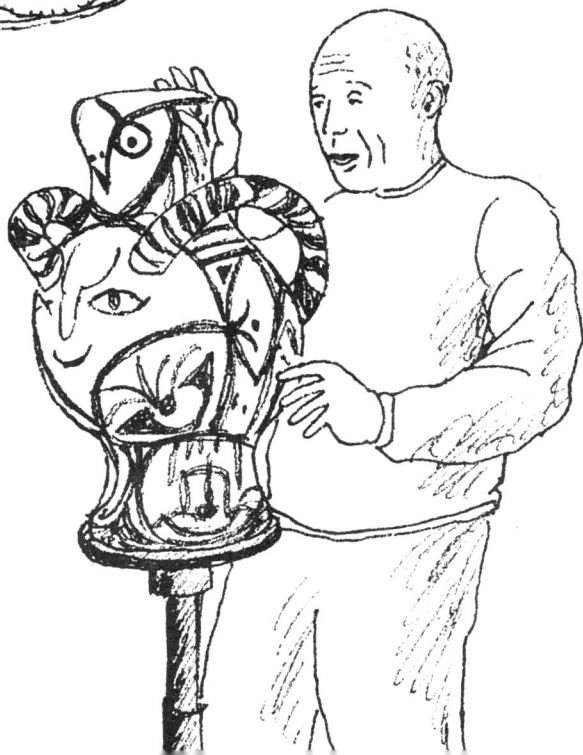

在自家的工作室里，毕加索致力于创作好玩又充满童趣的雕塑。这些雕塑是用他在附近捡到的物品做成的，所以它们被称为"拾得物艺术"。毕加索在垃圾场看见地上扔着一个自行车的车座和两个车把手。他把它们焊接在一起。就这样，它们顿时看起来就像一个牛头了！

1943年创作的《牛头》

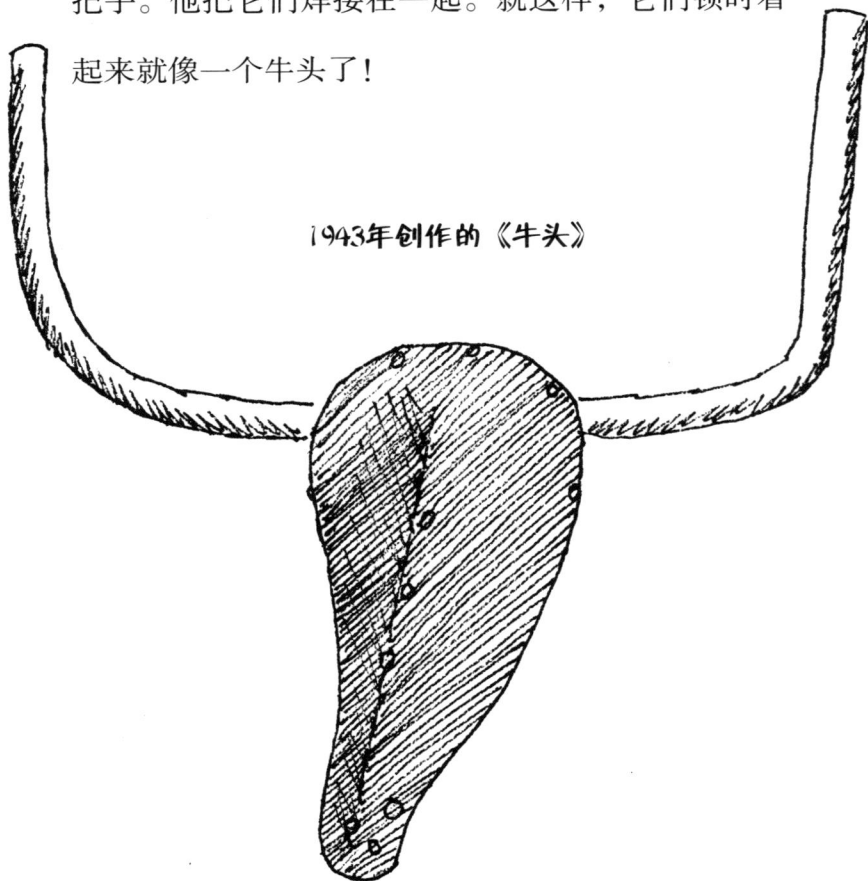

为了做一个推婴儿车的
女人的雕塑，毕加索使用了
真正的婴儿车上的零部件和
蛋糕烤盘。

1950年创作的
《推婴儿车的女人》

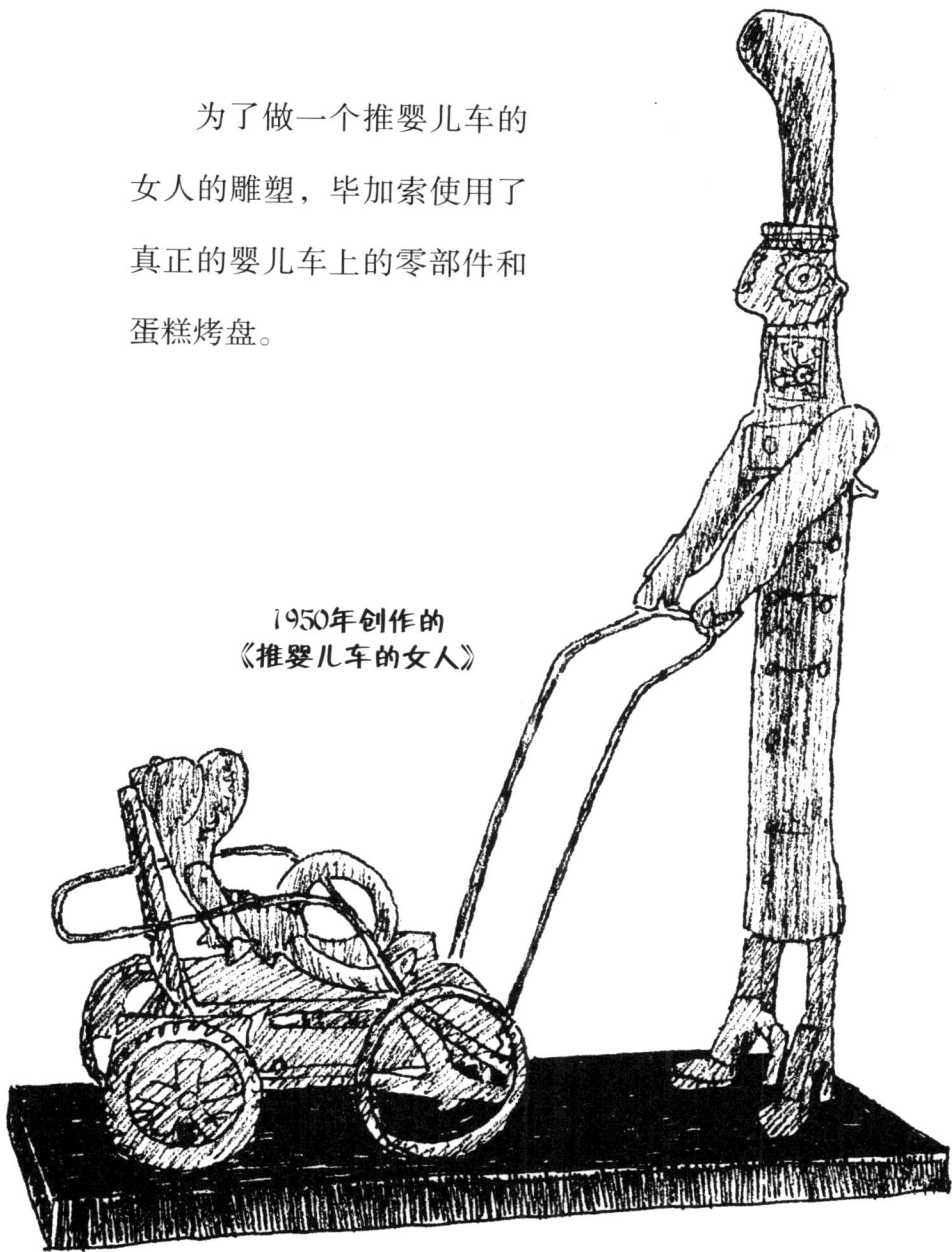

毕加索的一些雕塑会让人捧腹大笑。在塑造一只猿的时候，毕加索用一辆玩具汽车做猿脸，用一根汽车弹簧做尾巴，用一个水罐做身体，再用咖啡杯把手做耳朵。

1952年创作的
《母猿和它的幼崽》

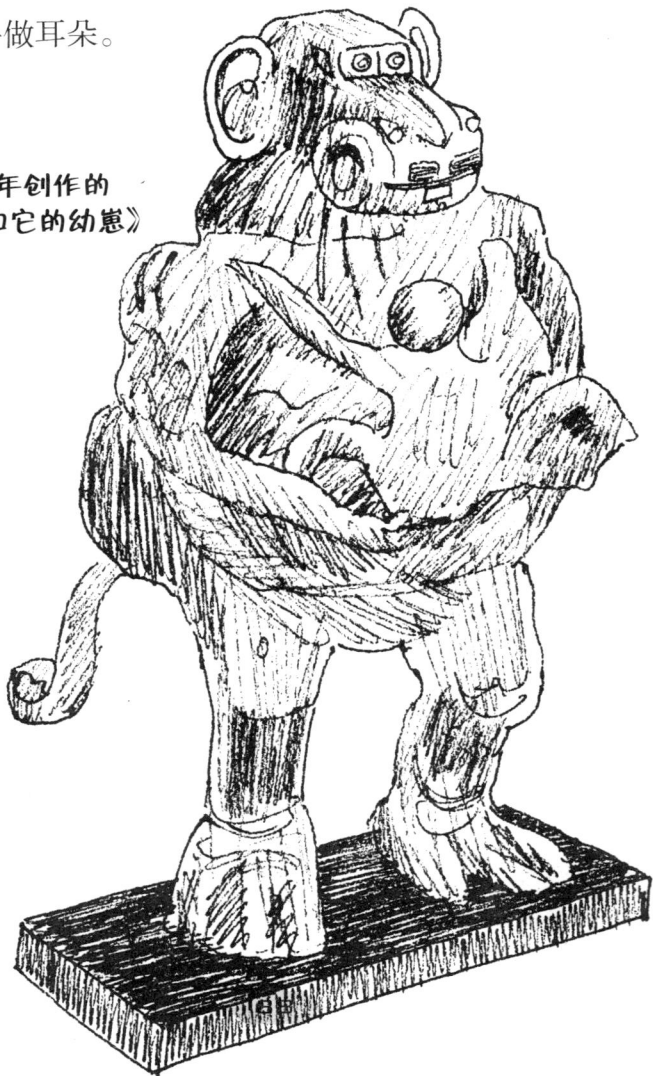

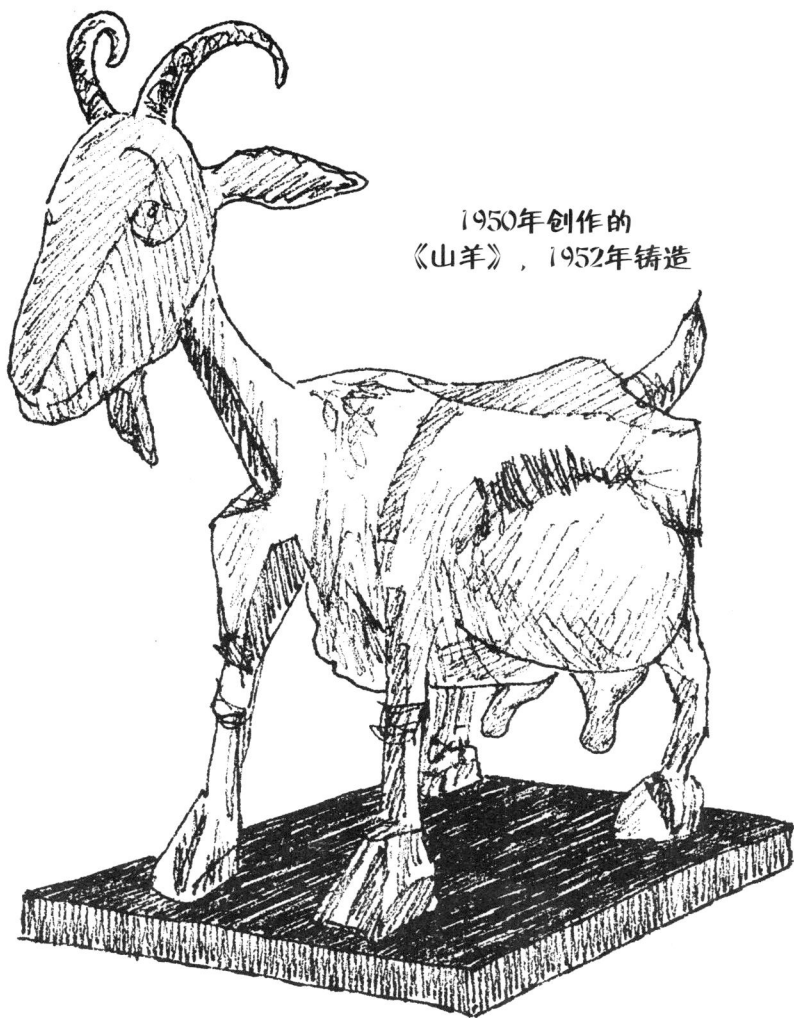

1950年创作的
《山羊》，1952年铸造

他还用花盆、篮子和棕榈叶制作了一个山羊雕塑。

此时，毕加索成了一个幸福的顾家男人。他花很多时间和他的孩子在一起，教他们游泳、做游戏、画画。他似乎沉浸在宁静的生活中。可是这种宁静会一直持续下去吗？不会！

毕加索、克劳德和帕洛玛

第九章　忙碌的晚年

1950年左右，
在工作室里

1953 年，在毕加索七十一岁的时候，弗朗索瓦丝离开了他。他简直不敢相信这是真的！以前还没有哪个女人离开过他，向来都是他先提出分手。弗朗索瓦丝把两个孩子也带走了，这对毕加索是一个沉重的打击。不久之后，他的画家朋友亨利·马蒂斯去世了，这对他又是一个打击。

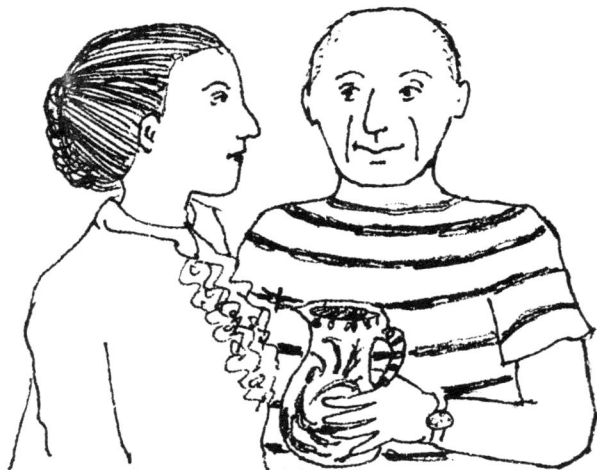

不过，毕加索又获得了一次拥抱浪漫爱情的机会！他在陶艺厂遇到了一位名叫杰奎琳·罗克的女子。直到毕加索去世，她一直深爱着他。他们结婚的时候，毕加索已经八十岁了！毕加索和杰奎琳生活在法国南部的豪宅里。毕加索以自己的画室和杰奎琳为题材画了许多画，他至少为杰奎琳画了一百五十幅肖像画。他还创作了一组名为"画家和模特儿系列"的画。他一直在进行艺术实验和探索。毕加索说："我的时间越来越少，但我想表达的东西却越来越多。"

他有一个计划是研究其他艺术家的经典名作，

比如西班牙画家委拉斯开兹的作品，然后用他自己的风格来重画这些画。毕加索似乎想以重画名画的方式来理解艺术史。

1656年迭戈·委拉斯开兹创作的《宫娥》

1957年毕加索创作的《宫娥》

毕加索以这个为主题创作了五十八幅画！

时至今日，毕加索的艺术作品已经在世界各地展出过了。他声名显赫，因而很难有隐私。他和杰奎琳搬到法国南部山区一座僻静的别墅里。他的别墅安装了电动门，还养了警犬。即使是他的孩子要进来见他也不容易。

在他八十五岁生日那天，巴黎多家博物馆纷纷举办毕加索作品展，以此向他致敬，展出的作品共有一千件之多。

毕加索仍然在创作。甚至九十一岁时，他还在进行艺术实验。他开始制作麻胶版画。

1961年创作的金属板雕塑《足球运动员》，高四米六

他还用上过颜色的金属板创作了一种新型雕塑。他每天仍然可以完成三四幅甚至五幅画！

有时，毕加索让人觉得他好像会永远活下去。

如何制作麻胶版画

1. 将你的图案反着画在麻胶板上。

2. 沿着你画的线条雕刻，将希望给纸印出颜色的位置上的麻胶割去。

3. 用手推墨辊或滚筒给麻胶板涂上油墨。

4. 把纸铺在麻胶板上，用塑料匙轻抹。

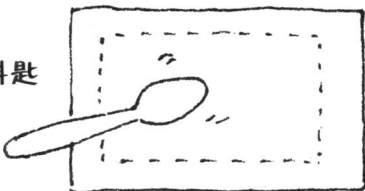

瞧！

然而，1973 年 4 月 8 日，巴勃罗·毕加索的心脏最终停止了跳动。陪在他床边的医生听到了他最后的话："你不应该不结婚，结婚是好事。"这就是毕加索，直到最后一刻都如此出人意料。

现在有博物馆专门陈列毕加索的艺术作品，其中一家在巴塞罗那，一家在巴黎。

毕加索留下了数量庞大的作品，可能有五万件之多。不过，让人们觉得不可思议的并不是他作品的数量，令人叹为观止的是他的天赋。一个人怎么会有这么充沛的精力？一个人怎么会有这么多奇思妙想？一个人怎么会活得这么充实？毕加索留给世界的财富是他的艺术，但他同时也展示了一个人如何用充沛的精力、独创精神和满腔热情来过一种极具创意的生活。

毕加索八十八至九十一岁完成的作品！

1969年

| 165幅油画 | 45幅素描 |

1970年至1972年3月

156幅雕版画

1970年

194幅素描

1971年11月至1972年8月

172幅素描

1970年9月至1972年6月

201幅绘画

1972年，毕加索最后
一幅自画像

毕加索年表

1881	10 月 25 日出生
1889	八岁时画了第一幅油画
1895	搬到巴塞罗那，进入美术学院学习
1900	在四只猫咖啡馆举办首场画展
1901	卡萨吉马斯自杀身亡；蓝色时期开始；1901 至 1904 年期间，辗转往返于西班牙和法国之间
1906	创作肖像画《格特鲁德·斯泰因》；结识马蒂斯和布拉克
1912	创作第一批拼贴画
1921	妻子奥尔加·霍赫洛娃生下儿子保罗
1925	举办首场超现实主义画展
1937	创作《格尔尼卡》
1947	弗朗索瓦丝·吉洛生下儿子克劳德；开始制作陶器
1949	设计了作为和平象征的鸽子；弗朗索瓦丝生下女儿帕洛玛
1954	马蒂斯去世
1961	娶杰奎琳为妻；制作波状金属雕塑
1966	在毕加索八十五岁生日那天，巴黎展出了他的一千件作品
1973	4 月 8 日去世，享年九十一岁

世界大事年表

阿尔伯特·爱因斯坦诞生 —— 1879

巴黎举办世界博览会 —— 1900

莱特兄弟在美国北卡罗来纳州小鹰市驾驶 —— 1903
飞机飞行成功

4月14日，泰坦尼克号在首航中沉没 —— 1912

第一次世界大战爆发 —— 1914

第一次世界大战结束；全球大流感造成两千万 —— 1918
至四千万人死亡

纽约股票市场崩盘，引发了经济大萧条 —— 1929

阿道夫·希特勒成为纳粹德国的总理 —— 1933

西班牙内战爆发，持续了三年 —— 1936

第二次世界大战爆发 —— 1939

美国向日本两座城市投下原子弹； —— 1945
第二次世界大战结束

"猫王"埃尔维斯·普莱斯利以《伤心旅店》 —— 1956
首次创下销量冠军记录

"阿波罗11号"飞船的指挥官尼尔·阿姆斯特朗 —— 1969
成为第一位登月的宇航员

理查德·M.尼克松辞去美国总统职务 —— 1974

英文朗读 CD 目录

Track 1 Who Was Pablo Picasso?

Track 2 Chapter 1 The Boy Wonder

Track 3 Pablo's life in Spain

Track 4 Chapter 2 The Young Artist

Track 5 Chapter 3 Life in Paris

Track 6 Les Saltimbanques & Picasso's Pets & Portrait of
         Gertrude Stein

Track 7 Chapter 4 Pablo's Shocking Paintings

Track 8 Les Demoiselles d'Avignon

Track 9 Chapter 5 Something New

Track 10 Chapter 6 Falling in Love Again and Again

Track 11 Making an Etching & Picasso's Muses…The Women
          in His Life

Track 12 Chapter 7 War and Peace

Track 13 Chapter 8 Pots and Pans

Track 14 Chapter 9 Busy to the End

Track 15 How to Make a Linoleum Block Print

Track 16 Timelines of Pablo Picasso's Life & the World

Who Was
Pablo Picasso?

Written and illustrated

by True Kelley

With thanks to the public libraries in Concord

and Warner, New Hampshire

——T.K.

Who Was Pablo Picasso?

If you think about modern art, Picasso is probably the first name that pops into your head. Art today wouldn't be the same without him!

Pablo Picasso had a very long and interesting life. He lived through two world wars, the invention of electricity, telephones, radio and TV, movies, automobiles, and airplanes. As the world changed, he was able to change with it.

Picasso made all kinds of art and plenty of it. He worked hard every day for more than eighty years. Some people say he created 50,000 pieces of art! He must have had tons of energy.

He made paintings, posters, sculptures in stone and metal, ceramics, drawings, collages, prints, poetry, theater sets, costumes, and more. Picasso kept thinking of new ideas. He was creative and skilled, but as soon as he mastered a certain style, he'd move on. As a result, the way he painted changed more than any other great artist.

Unlike many artists, Picasso was successful and became famous quite quickly. He always knew how to attract attention. At nine years old, Picasso was selling his drawings. By the time he died at age ninety-one, he was the richest artist in history.

Through his art, Picasso sent powerful messages about politics, society, peace, and love. Because of

Picasso, the dove is considered a symbol of peace. And his most famous painting, *Guernica,* shows the horror and <u>brutality</u> of war.

Picasso's art could be serious or playful, childlike or realistic, colorful or dark, simple or complex. When he was a child, he could draw as well as a talented grown-up. But the older he got, the more he wanted to make art like a child.

Chapter 1
The Boy Wonder

On October 25, 1881, in Malaga in southern Spain, an art teacher and his wife had a baby boy. They named him after many saints and relatives: Pablo Diego Jose Francisco de Paula Juan Nepomuceno Maria de los Remedios Cipriano de la Santisima Trinidad Ruiz y Picasso. Years later that baby became known as the great artist, Pablo Picasso. How would he ever have signed his whole name on a painting? It would have been impossible!

So he just wrote "Picasso."

Pablo could draw before he could talk. His mother said his first words were "Piz! Piz!" That's baby talk in Spanish for *lapiz*, which means "pencil." When he was really little, he liked to draw spirals. He would sometimes draw pictures in the sand.

If he drew a horse, he could start from any point—the tail or the leg—and make a very good picture in one line. He could do the same with paper and scissors. Have you ever tried to do that? It's not easy!

Pablo's parents wanted him to be an artist. As a little boy, he often went to bullfights with his father. Pablo's first known painting was of a bullfight. He was only about eight years old when he did it. Everyone thought Pablo was an artistic genius— and they were right.

Pablo had two younger sisters, Lola and Conchita. Sadly, when Pablo was still young, seven-year-old Conchita died of diphtheria. The whole family was crushed. For the rest of his life, Pablo had a fear of death.

When Pablo was thirteen, he had his first art show. By then, his father saw that Pablo painted better than he did. So Pablo's father gave his son all his brushes and paints and never painted again.

Pablo and his family moved to Barcelona, an exciting city full of artists. Pablo was accepted to the local art school where his father taught drawing. Even though he was only fourteen, Pablo skipped the basic courses and went right to the advanced ones. He amazed the teachers!

Pablo's career really began when he was

sixteen. He did a painting called *Science and Charity*. His father and sister Lola were his models. Lola was shown sick in bed. Pablo's father posed as the doctor at her bedside. The painting was very realistic in style. It won a prize at an exhibit in Madrid. Pablo beat some of the best artists in Spain!

Pablo's family thought he had a great future as an artist. They sent him to Madrid to study art at the Royal Academy of San Fernando. It was supposed to be a good school, but Pablo skipped class a lot. His teachers wanted him to copy other paintings and statues. He thought this way of teaching was useless and old-fashioned. He ended up spending a lot of time goofing off in cafés. He also loved going to the famous Prado Art Museum, where he saw the work of the Spanish masters El Greco and Francisco Goya.

In the winter, Pablo came down with scarlet fever. He left school and stayed in a country village until he got better. He had a lot of time to think about his future. Pablo decided not to go back to school. He also decided that he wanted to paint his own way. His family was not going to like that, but Pablo was <u>restless</u> and ready to be on his own.

Pablo's life in Spain

Pablo and his family moved from Malaga in southern Spain, where he was born, to La Coruña in northern Spain, and then to Barcelona. After that, Pablo went to Madrid to study art. When he became sick, he went to the little village of Horta de San Juan. He later returned to Barcelona, but he couldn't resist Paris.

Chapter 2
The Young Artist

Pablo moved back to Barcelona where he hung out with a bunch of artists, poets, and writers at a café called Els Quatre Gats ("The Four Cats"). They called themselves "Modernistes"—modern artists. In 1900, Pablo had his first one-man show at the café. There were more than fifty portraits of friends and family and another sixty or so drawings and paintings. One was a painting of a priest at the bedside of a dying woman. It was accepted for a show at the World's Fair in Paris. It was all Pablo needed as an excuse to move to Paris. An old art school friend, Carles Casagemas, went with him.

Carles and Pablo had no money. Their apartment had no furniture so Pablo painted furniture and bookcases on the walls. Then it didn't look so bare. He even painted a safe on the wall as if they had valuable things to put in it.

But the apartment didn't matter. They were in Paris! It was the center of the art and fashion world. Paris was full of life, and Picasso was full of energy! He was seeing the art of Monet, Degas, Cezanne, Van Gogh, Gauguin, and Toulouse-Lautrec. Paris was so colorful, and soon so were Pablo's paintings. For two months, he painted Paris scenes. He sold three pastels of bullfights. That was encouraging.

Pablo loved Paris. But poor Carles was brokenhearted. His girlfriend had left him. So Carles and Pablo moved back to Pablo's hometown in Spain. Pablo's family did not like what they saw when he walked in the door! The way he was dressed! And his long hair! They were sure he was wasting his life.

So Pablo moved to Madrid. He helped start an art magazine. He did political cartoons for the magazine about the sorry state of the poor. He left behind his friend Carles, who was still terribly depressed and difficult to be around. Soon Carles Casagemas returned to Paris. He was at his wits' end. First he tried to shoot his old girlfriend. Then he shot himself and died.

Pablo was in shock. He may have also felt guilty about leaving his friend in such bad shape. Carles's death affected Picasso's painting. He painted two dark funeral scenes and two death portraits of Carles. Then he began painting with the color blue.

Pablo said, "It was thinking of Casagemas that made me start painting in blue." He did a self-portrait in 1901 that was mostly in blues. It made him look very sad. Later, this time became known as Picasso's Blue Period.

From 1901 to 1904, Pablo moved back and forth between Barcelona and Paris. He lived in cheap hotel rooms and <u>run-down</u> apartments. Pablo shared one apartment with Max Jacob, a poet. They could only afford one bed, so Pablo slept in it during the day, and Max slept in it at night. Pablo worked at night, a habit that continued for the rest of his life.

Because he often couldn't afford to buy canvases and paints, Pablo did lots of drawings. His subjects were beggars, blind people, lonely people, and prisoners. Pablo cared about these people. For models, he visited a women's prison in Paris. All his life, Pablo loved painting women.

It was 1903. In only a little over a year, Pablo did fifty paintings using tones of blue and green. No one bought them. People didn't want to put such depressing pictures on their walls. Pablo's dad and a lot of his friends were sure Pablo was headed in the wrong direction with his strange blue paintings. But did Pablo listen? No. He did what he wanted!

Chapter 3
Life in Paris

What made Pablo snap out of his Blue Period? Moving back to Paris—this time for good—was one cause. Lively Paris worked its magic on Pablo. He became happier. He started doing colorful paintings of jugglers and acrobats in a traveling circus. They were all outsiders to society, just like the people he had painted in his Blue Period.

The other reason that his Blue Period ended was Pablo had a new girlfriend. She was a beautiful artist named Fernande Olivier. His happiness showed in his paintings. This time in Pablo's life is sometimes called the Rose Period, but his paintings had many colors. Not just pinks.

Les Saltimbanques

Pablo worked hard on his painting, *Les Saltimbanques (The Family of Acrobats)*. He used both Fernande and a friend as models for the circus family. X-ray studies of the painting show that he did the painting completely over four times until he had it the way he wanted.

Picasso's Pets

Throughout his life, Pablo had many pets, including a tame white mouse, a tortoise, a goat, and a monkey. He was a true dog lover. When he was still a struggling artist, he had a big, sweet, old dog named Frika. Once when Pablo had no food, Frika trotted in dragging a string of sausages! His all-time favorite pet was probably a dachshund named Lump. Lump means "rascal" in German. Pablo painted Lump into his copy of *Las Meninas* instead of the noble-looking hound that Velázquez painted in the original.

Pablo and Fernande lived in a big, run-down apartment building that was full of artists and poets. Their room was damp and a mess with lots of projects going on. Pablo didn't like to throw out anything. He said, "Why should you want me to throw away what has done me the favor of coming into my hands?"

They had a big, yellow dog named Frika, and they kept a pet white mouse in a dresser drawer. Pablo liked to work at night by oil lamp. He often worked until five or six in the morning. In winter, the room was sometimes so cold that leftover cups of tea froze overnight.

Around this time, Pablo was meeting lots of interesting people in Paris. They thought he was interesting, too. He was intense and complicated. He could be very charming and his curiosity, energy, intellect, and originality caught people's attention. Despite being short, only five feet three inches tall, he was very striking-looking with piercing black eyes.

He met a rich American woman named Gertrude Stein and her brother Leo. Gertrude was a poet. She had written the famous line, "Rose is a rose is a rose is a rose." She was one of the first people to really appreciate Pablo's paintings, and she bought some of them.

Poets and artists met at the Steins's house in Paris on Saturday nights. Pablo met the painter Henri Matisse there. Pablo thought Matisse was the greatest painter of the time. "All things considered, there is only Matisse," he once said. Even though they were competitors, they became lifelong friends.

After working on a portrait of Gertrude Stein, Pablo realized that he didn't have to paint exactly what he saw. He could paint what he imagined. This led to a turning point for Pablo. It was a turning point in the history of modern art!

Portrait of Gertrude Stein

In 1906, Pablo worked on a portrait of Gertrude. It was torture for Pablo because he just couldn't get her face right. She sat for the portrait eighty times! It probably was torture for Gertrude, too! Pablo gave up for the summer; in the fall, he painted in her face from memory. It looked like a primitive mask. Pablo had been looking at African and primitive art in a museum, which explains why. He was never afraid to borrow ideas.

People didn't think the painting looked like Gertrude at all, but she loved it. She said, "For me, it is I."

Chapter 4
Pablo's Shocking Paintings

In 1907, Pablo painted the biggest painting he had ever done: eight feet tall and eight feet wide. It showed five women, one whose head looked like it was on backward. The painting was called *Les Demoiselles D'Avignon*.

Everyone hated it! One critic said it was "the work of a madman." Pablo put it away and didn't show it again for nine years. It was fun to get the attention, but his feelings were hurt.

Today it has been called the first modern twentieth century painting. Picasso had found a new way of seeing.

There was one person who really liked Pablo's experimental style. He was an art gallery owner named D. H. Kahnweiler. He became Pablo's art dealer and close friend.

Another close friend was the artist Georges Braque. Picasso and Braque found that they thought alike. They were both influenced by the paintings of Paul Cezanne.

For five years, Braque and Picasso saw each other every day. They even went on vacation together. They worked together so closely that Pablo said, at times, they couldn't tell who had painted which painting. They would also look at each other's work and decide together if a painting was finished. Braque said he and Picasso were like mountain climbers attached to the same rope. Pablo never again worked so closely with another artist.

Braque and Picasso did still life paintings, landscapes, and portraits. They both used only a few colors and broke up objects in the paintings into cubes and geometric shapes. They were trying to paint their subjects from all sides at once. Pablo said, "I paint objects as I think them, not as I see them." Together, they were inventing a new style—cubism!

Of all the important artwork that Pablo created in his life, it was cubism that made him famous. At first people were shocked by cubism. They had never seen anything like it. But soon people realized they liked it!

Pablo said, "I knew we were painting strange things, but the world seemed a strange place to us."

Les Demoiselles d'Avignon

The painting was really wild by the standards of the day. The five women in the painting look very angular and distorted. They are ugly! They seem to be breaking into pieces.

People thought the painting should look more real. This was <u>upsetting</u>! Shocking! No one had ever done a painting like it. Creating it changed Pablo's understanding of painting. Pablo had taken many months to paint this picture. He had done many, many sketches for it (eight hundred and nine!). He knew he was breaking all the rules, but he was trying to paint the women from more than one angle at a time as if the viewer was seeing them from many different sides all at once.

Chapter 5
Something New

By 1909, Pablo was becoming well-known. His paintings were different, but people were buying them. He and Fernande moved into a fancier house. They hired a maid. They spent the summer with Braque in an old villa in the mountains. Then he and Fernande broke up. Pablo said, "Her beauty held me, but I could not stand any of her little ways."

Soon Pablo had a new girlfriend, Eva Gouel. Pablo painted a picture of Eva, called *Ma Jolie,* which means "My Pretty Girl." Pablo was in love again. He fell in love many times in his long life.

Once again Picasso and Braque were on to something new. They started using stencils and printed words in their paintings. They also began pasting things on to their pictures. If they wanted a newspaper to be shown, instead of painting it, they stuck on a real piece of newspaper. That was how collage began. Collage means "to stick." One of Pablo's first collages was called *Still Life with Chair Caning.*

Braque and Picasso went on, in their playful way, sticking other things onto their paintings—pieces of cloth, sandpaper, wallpaper, even trash!

But their experiments with art were <u>interrupted</u> by world events. In 1914, a local war between

Austria-Hungary and Serbia grew into what became known as the Great War—World War I. The Archduke of Austria was killed by a Serb. Germany backed Austria-Hungary and Russia backed Serbia. Germany declared war on Russia, and then on France. Soon countries all over the world were involved, including the United States.

In 1914, Braque was drafted into the French army. Pablo wasn't a French citizen. He didn't have to join the army. He stayed in Paris while many of his friends went off to fight. Pablo missed them.

France was fighting against Germany. Because Pablo's friend, the gallery owner Kahnweiler, was German, he was forced to leave France. (The French thought anybody German was an enemy.) The gallery was closed by the French authorities.

All of Pablo's work there was <u>confiscated</u>.

In 1915 Pablo's dear Eva died of tuberculosis. Pablo was brokenhearted. Again his sadness showed in his paintings. He had worked on one painting while Eva was sick, *Harlequin,* and finished it after she died. It shows a clownlike artist in front of an easel holding an unfinished painting. The background is black. It was a bleak time in Europe and in Pablo's personal life as well.

Chapter 6
Falling in Love Again and Again

During World War I, Pablo found some new friends in Paris. One of them was a poet and playwright named Jean Cocteau. He introduced Pablo to a music composer. The two of them convinced Pablo to design a set and costumes for a ballet to be performed in Rome. It was about a circus and was called *Parade*. Pablo had never even seen a ballet before! He traveled to Rome to work on it. When it was finally performed, *Parade* bombed. It was too different for most people. The costumes were wild. So were the sets... and the music... and the dancing.

While in Rome, Pablo became fascinated with ancient Greek and Roman art. He also became fascinated with beautiful Olga Khokhlova, one of the dancers in the ballet. He married her a year later.

Back in Paris, Olga introduced Pablo to high society. They went to formal balls and to fancy resorts. For someone like Pablo who had always cared so much about the poor, this was quite a switch. Olga was a snob. She kept Picasso away from old friends, and Pablo went along with it. He didn't need to work anymore. He was already rich. Yet that didn't mean he stopped working. Once again, he just changed direction.

After the war, Pablo did far less with cubism and collage. He went back to painting in more traditional ways. After all his experimenting, Pablo had found another way to surprise people... by not being the Picasso they expected!

In 1921, Pablo and Olga had a son, Paulo. Pablo adored his new baby. He loved being a father, but it was a big change for him.

Over and over he painted mother and son in a new style. The forms were solid-looking, not jagged and broken as in his cubist paintings.

His painting, *Three Women at the Spring*, shows three figures in classical Greek style clothing. They have very rounded forms and thick legs. Picasso said painting the legs brought back childhood memories of crawling under the dinner table and seeing his aunts' ankles.

At the same time he also painted *Three Musicians* in a very simplified cubist style. But now the shapes and colors were brighter. The figures looked like pieces in a jigsaw puzzle. Why would Picasso change suddenly from one style to another? He said he was simply using the style that best suited the subject.

Then Pablo started painting things like centaurs and fauns. He had admired them in the ancient statues and art that he had seen in Italy.

The cubists thought Picasso was selling out. Picasso didn't care what other artists thought. He didn't want to be <u>label</u>ed. He was Picasso!

By 1925, Picasso became interested in the surrealist movement in art and literature. Surrealist painting was a way of expressing the unconscious mind.

Picasso painted a world of dreams and nightmares. He took part in a show of surrealist art. On the side, Picasso was also writing poetry and doing book illustrations and etchings. He had enough energy for ten people!

Many of Picasso's surrealistic drawings and etchings were about bullfighting. He also made many images of the Minotaur, an imaginary creature that was half man and half bull. Some art critics think that Picasso liked to think of himself as a Minotaur!

Picasso also became interested in making sculpture. He had done some collage paintings of a guitar that used many 3-D objects—nails, string, and a cloth. It was as if paintings like this were becoming sculptures.

One day Picasso met a metalworker and sculptor in Paris. His name was Julio Gonzales. He was Spanish, too. Julio and Pablo became friends. They worked together on abstract sculptures using welded metal rods and wire. It was something completely new.

Unfortunately, Pablo's marriage to Olga was falling apart. They were living on separate floors of their house. She hated his messy studio (and it was messy!). Pablo said the mess inspired him. Olga was the problem. "She asked too much of me," he said. So he bought a grand house north of Paris to escape her. Picasso said his last months with Olga were a nightmare.

At his new place Picasso set up a sculpture studio in the stables. He made big plaster heads and started doing sculpture made with odd materials. One sculpture, *Head of a Woman*, was made using colanders.

Picasso met a young girl just as she was coming out of the subway in Paris. Her name was Marie-Therese Walter. It was love at first sight. Immediately Picasso began painting her. Years later, he and Marie-Therese had a child together, a girl named Maya. Did they live happily ever after? No!

Picasso met a photographer named Dora Maar. He fell in love with her just a year after his daughter was born. Picasso seemed to enjoy having a very complicated love life. He was still seeing Marie-Therese and still dealing with Olga, and now there was Dora.

Making an Etching

Etchings are drawings scratched with a sharp tool on a metal plate. Prints are then made from the plate.

1. Cut design in copper plate treated with acid resist.

2. Wash design with acid which will eat into the cuts. (The acid resist protects other areas.)

3. Roll on ink and wipe off excess ink so ink stays only in the cuts.

4. Print. Lines holding the ink make the image.

Picasso's Muses...

The Women in His Life

Women were attracted to Picasso, but he must have been difficult to live with! He had a temper and could be grumpy when his work wasn't going well. Of course, he was totally charming at other times. He loved women, but he was very self-centered and absorbed by his art. In his life he had many girlfriends and wives, and four children. They were important to him as models and as his greatest source of inspiration. We know what the women looked like because he drew and painted them all. They were all beautiful.

Chapter 7
War and Peace

Some artists work on one idea and in one style. But Picasso changed all the time. Picasso's paintings reflected what was going on in his personal life as well as what was happening in the outside world.

In 1936 the Spanish Civil War broke out. Picasso was living in Paris, yet he was deeply affected by the war in Spain. He was a Spaniard, after all.

In Spain, a Republican government had been elected. But it was overthrown by General Francisco Franco and his forces. Franco was a dictator and ruled Spain until his death in 1975. Because of Franco, Picasso never returned to his native country.

In April, 1937, the town of *Guernica* in northeast Spain was bombed by the Germans who were helping Franco and his men. Guernica was not far from where Picasso grew up. The bombs fell on market day. More than sixteen hundred people— men, women, and children— were killed. Almost nine hundred more were injured. There was no military reason for the attack.

Picasso was <u>outraged</u> by the murder of all these innocent people. With all his passion, he painted a huge twelve-foot-high-by-twenty-six-foot-long painting called *Guernica.* It is his most famous painting. He finished it in just three weeks. His new girlfriend, Dora, took many photographs of him working on it.

In gray tones, the painting shows a screaming horse, a fallen soldier, a screaming woman on fire falling from a burning house, and a mother holding her dead baby. There's a cutoff arm holding a sword and a severed head. There is a bull amid the chaos, which may symbolize the hope of overcoming Franco. *Guernica* is a very strong and disturbing portrayal of the horrors of war.

When he was asked to explain the painting, Picasso said, "It isn't up to the painter to define the symbols. Otherwise, it would be better if he wrote them out in so many words!"

Then, in 1939, World War II started after the German army invaded Poland. Fearing bombings, museums in Paris closed down. Much of the art was moved and hidden in the countryside. Many artists fled the city. So did Picasso with his family. They moved to Royan, a small town in France on the Atlantic coast.

In 1940, the Germans occupied Paris. Picasso decided to move back to his studio there. Why? Perhaps Picasso hoped his presence would be a proud symbol to the French of defiance and freedom.

It was hard to get food. So sometimes Picasso painted pictures of sausages and leeks. Art supplies were also scarce. Even so, Picasso managed to paint every day. He also wrote a play. The Nazis did not approve of any of his work. But that didn't stop Picasso!

Picasso's love for Dora was fading. He met a young artist, Françoise Gilot, and began a ten-year-long romance with her.

In 1944, the Nazis were finally driven out of Paris. Picasso kept on painting. He sang loudly while he worked to drown out the sounds of the gunfire. As soon as the Germans were gone, Paris had a party. The city was free again. The war was almost over.

American soldiers poured into Paris. Some said the two things they most wanted to do were see the Eiffel Tower and meet Picasso! Picasso was pleased to give tours of his studio. Everyone was welcome. Some soldiers arrived so tired, they fell asleep there. Once someone counted twenty sleeping men in the studio!

The Second World War lasted six years. Picasso had now lived through three wars. He knew how important it was to work for peace. In 1948, he went to the Peace Congress in Poland. The following year, he made a poster of a dove for the Peace Congress. Because of Picasso, the dove has become a symbol for peace all over the world.

Chapter 8
Pots and Pans

After the war, Picasso and Françoise moved to the town of Vallauris in southern France. They lived in an old perfume factory with room for a sculpture studio. Their two children were born in Vallauris—a son, Claude, in 1947 and a daughter, Paloma (which means "dove"), in 1949.

There was also a pottery factory in town. Picasso began working with the potters, making and decorating ceramics, plates, and vases.

At first he just decorated pieces made by the potters. But soon he was making pottery himself. His designs were happy and playful.

At home in his studio, Picasso worked on amusing and childlike sculptures. They were made from things he found around the place. And so the pieces were called "Found Art." At a junkyard, Picasso saw a bicycle seat and handlebars lying next to each other. He welded them together. Suddenly they looked exactly like a bull's head!

For a sculpture of a woman pushing a baby carriage, Picasso used parts from a real baby carriage and cake pans.

Some of his sculptures would make you laugh. For an ape, Picasso used a toy car for a face, a car spring for a tail, a jug for a body, and coffee cup handles for ears.

He made a sculpture of a goat out of flowerpots, a basket, and palm leaves.

Pablo was now a happy family man. He spent time with his children, teaching them to swim, playing, and drawing with them. He seemed to have found peace in his life. But did it last? No!

Chapter 9
Busy to the End

In 1953, when Picasso was seventy-one years old, Françoise left him. He couldn't believe it! No woman had ever left him before. He had always been the one to call it quits. Françoise took the children with her. That was a huge blow to Pablo. His friend, the artist Henri Matisse, died a little while later. Another blow.

But leave it to Picasso to find romance again! He met a woman, Jacqueline Roque, at the pottery factory. She was devoted to him until the day he died. They got married when Pablo was eighty years old! Pablo and Jacqueline lived in luxurious houses in southern France. Picasso painted pictures of his studio and of Jacqueline. He did at least one hundred and fifty portraits of her. He did a group of pictures called "The Artist and Model Series." He kept experimenting and exploring. Picasso said, "I have less and less time and yet, I have more and more to say."

One of his projects was to look at old masterpieces by other artists, such as the Spanish painter Velázquez, and translate the paintings into his own style. Picasso seemed to be trying to understand the history of art by redoing it in his own way.

By now there were shows of his art all over the world. He was such a celebrity that it was hard to have any privacy. He and Jacqueline moved to a secluded villa in the hills of southern France. His villa had electronic gates and guard dogs. Even his own children had trouble getting in to see him.

On his eighty-fifth birthday, museums in Paris honored Picasso with shows of his work—a thousand pieces in all.

And still Picasso kept working. Even at ninety-one he was experimenting. He started making linoleum block prints.

He also made a new kind of sculpture with painted sheet metal. He would still turn out three, four, or even five paintings a day!

Sometimes it seemed as if Picasso would go on

forever. However, on April 8, 1973, Pablo Picasso's heart finally gave out. The doctor by his bedside heard his last words: "You are wrong not to be married. It's useful." That was Picasso, surprising to the end.

Several museums are now devoted to his art—including one in Barcelona and one in Paris.

He left behind a huge body of work. There may be as many as fifty thousand pieces. But it is not the quantity of art that <u>boggles</u> the mind. It is his genius that is so amazing. How could one man have so much energy? How could one man come up with so many new ideas? How could one man have lived so fully? Picasso's gift to the world was his art, but he also showed how a creative life could be when lived with energy, originality, and passion.

How to Make a Linoleum Block Print

1. Draw your design in reverse on a linoleum block.

2. Carve around your lines removing all linoleum where you want the color of the paper you print on.

3. Roll ink on block with a brayer or roller.

4. Place paper over block. Run with a plastic spoon.

Timeline of Pablo Picasso's Life

1881 — Born October 25

1889 — Paints first oil painting, age eight

1895 — Moves to Barcelona and goes to School of Fine Arts

1900 — First show at Els Quatre Gats Café

1901 — Casagemas dies; Blue Period begins; moves back and forth between Spain and France, 1901-1904

1906 — Paints *Gertrude Stein*; meets Matisse and Braque

1912 — First collages

1921 — Son Paulo born to wife Olga Khokhlova

1925 — First surrealist show

1937 — Paints *Guernica*

1947 — Son Claude born to Françoise Gilot; begins making ceramics

1949 — Invents dove as peace symbol; daughter Paloma born to Françoise

1954 — Matisse dies

1961 — Marries Jacqueline; makes corrugated metal sculptures

1966 — One thousand works are shown in Paris for Picasso's eighty-fifth birthday

1973 — Dies April 8, age ninety-one

Timeline of the World

Albert Einstein is born — 1879

World's Fair in Paris — 1900

Wright brothers fly a plane at Kitty Hawk, North Carolina — 1903

The *Titanic* sinks on its very first voyage on April 14 — 1912

World War I starts — 1914

World War I ends; Great influenza epidemic kills an estimated — 1918
20-40 million people around the world

The New York stock market crashes, setting off the Great — 1929
Depression

Adolf Hitler becomes chancellor of Nazi Germany — 1933

Spanish Civil War begins and lasts for three years — 1936

World War II begins — 1939

United States drops atomic bombs on two Japanese cities; — 1945
World War II ends

Elvis Presley has his first number one hit record with — 1956
"Heartbreak Hotel"

Neil Armstrong, commander of *Apollo 11*, becomes first — 1969
astronaut to walk on the moon

Richard M. Nixon resigns as president of the United States — 1974

英文参考书目　Bibliography

Buchoholz, Elke Linda. Zimmermann, Beate. Ullmann, H.F.
Pablo Picasso: Life and Work. Konemann, Germany, 2008.

Green, Jen; Hughes, Andrew S.; Mason, Antony.
Famous Artists: Picasso. Barrons, New York, 1995.

Heslewood, Juliet. **Introducing Picasso.**
Little, Brown and Company, New York, 1993.

Kelley, True (Illustrator). **Pablo Picasso: Breaking All the Rules.** Penguin Group (USA), New York, 2002.

Leslie, Richard. **Pablo Picasso: A Modern Master.**
New Line Books, New York, 2006.

Meadows, Matthew. **Art for Young People: Pablo Picasso.**
Sterling Publishing, New York, 1996.

Scarborough, Kate. **Artists in Their Time: Pablo Picasso.**
Children's Press, New York, 2002.

Schaffner, Ingrid. **Essential Pablo Picasso.**
Harry Abrams, Inc. New York, 1999.

Warncke, Carsten-Peter. **Picasso.**
Taschen, London, 1998.

Wertenbaker, Lael. **The World of Picasso 1881-1973.**
Time-Life Books, New York, 1974.

词汇表 Vocabulary

英文	词性	中文	页码
amusing	*adj.*	好玩的、有趣的	P151
boggle	*vt.&vi.*	使惊奇、使困惑	P156
brutality	*n.*	残暴、无情、暴行	P109
charming	*adj.*	有魅力的、迷人的	P123
confiscate	*vt.*	没收、把……充公	P134
interrupt	*vt.&vi.*	打断、妨碍	P132
label	*vt.*	贴标签、把……归类	P138
nightmare	*n.*	噩梦、噩梦般的可怕处境	P139
outrage	*vt.*	使震怒、激怒	P145
restless	*adj.*	跃跃欲试的、焦躁不安的	P114
run-down	*adj.*	破旧的、破败的	P118
upsetting	*adj.*	令人不安、使人沮丧的	P129